Coach, There Is Hope!

ISBN **978-1-935786-93-1**

Printed in the United States of America
St. Clair Publications
P. O. Box 726
Mc Minnville, TN 37111-0726

http://stclairpublications.com

Cover Design

Kent Grey—Hesselbein Design Studio
www.kghdesignstudio.com

Front Cover Photo: Watson Brown
Complements, Coach Watson Brown

Coach, There is Hope!

Avoiding Stress and Burnout From the Things You Cannot Control

LaNise Rosemond, Ed.D

Coach Rose

Edited by Stanley J. St. Clair

CONTENTS

Acknowledgements

I want to thank the Lord for giving me insight on how to write this book. I also want to dedicate this book to Dad and Mom Collier for all your years of love, prayers, and encouragement. I appreciate you for the countless hours you have spent being my accountability partners and helping me develop and grow into the person I am today.

Furthermore, I want to thank my God parents, Dad and Mom Jackson, Dad and Mom Treece, and Dad and Mom Lloyd, for your love and support over the years.

Coach Watson Brown, you are my favorite coach in the NCAA! Thank you for dedicating over forty years to the coaching profession.

I want to thank Mr. Stanley St. Clair for everything he has done in assisting me with releasing this book. Jared Austin and Andrea Moran thank you for your professional assistance with this book.

Lastly, I want to thank Mrs. Miller, my second grade teacher, who used to look me in the eyes daily and tell me that one day I was going to do something so great!

LaNise

Introduction

America's fascination with sports has bridged the gap between people of all different types of socioeconomic backgrounds, races, genders, and ages. Individuals from various kinds of lifestyles can connect and share a unique bond over their love of a game. To ensure that our love of sports continues, we spend millions—even billions—of dollars on our favorite sports figures. We show our loyalty and our support through video games, apparel, sneakers, and even flags.

We love watching all types of athletes excel in their sports and we especially enjoy celebrating at the peak of an athlete's win if we know about his or her struggle to get to the top. It is not unusual for us to focus on certain athletes, especially if they have the ability to capture our imagination and inspire us through their creative athletic talents and personalities. Despite our focus on the individual athlete, most Americans overlook the person at the cornerstone of the sport, the person who unites a team and encourages those special individuals. That person is the coach.

This is not to say that Americans are unaware of coaches. We see them on television during sporting events and we see their tension, excitement and hopes for their athletes. We take note of their range of emotions and quick thinking during various plays. We hear their eloquent words during interviews, and we see their encouraging gestures that they freely give to their team players to reassure and boost their spirits. However, these observations are made in passing, as most of our attention is grabbed by the energy and excitement of the overcrowded stadiums, the mascots, the overzealous alumni, and the proud parents of the athletes. As a result, many do not consider the hard work that comes with the coaching profession. Undoubtedly, this is a very high-stress career, and if an individual lacks a proper balance or stress-relieving outlet, then it can and will lead to an early burnout.

According to Weinberg and Gould (2010)[1], burnout has been defined as an exhaustive psycho-physiological response exhibited as a result of frequent, sometimes extreme, and generally ineffective efforts to meet excessive competitive demands. These scholars described several symptoms of burnout: physical and mental exhaustion, lack of caring, lack of desire, loss of interest, depression, and increased anxiety. Additionally, burnout can involve an emotional, psychological, and sometimes physical withdrawal from a previously enjoyable activity in response to excessive stress or dissatisfaction over time (Smith, 1986)[1]. Weinberg and Gould (2010)[2] reiterated this by finding that when individuals reach burnout, they are more likely to withdraw from the stressful environment.

Stress in America's high schools, colleges, and professional sports are at an all-time high. Student athletes labor under the combined demands of academics and morning practices, evening practices, and study hall. On the other hand, coaches face extraordinary pressure from administration, alumni, and the public in regard to winning games. According to Weinberg and Gould (2010)[2], new and young coaches are experiencing the greatest amount of stress. Stress has become such an epidemic that it is now being identified as a health risk factor. They noted that coaches and athletes face similar stressors in competitive sports: long hours of practice, great physical and mental energy expenditure, and performance pressures on game day.

Upon receiving my first college job, the most common thing I would hear from people was that they wished that they had my job. People perceived my job as being easy because they thought I threw a ball to my athletes when they were out on the court, and they thought I stood around while watching athletes demonstrate their athletic talent.

People would often make comments indicating jealousy or envy, such as, "You get to travel all over the country" or "You get to exercise with your team since you can practice with your athletes" and "You get to be in the limelight." All of these comments can be true at times; however, they come at a great cost. There is no doubt that there are perks to being a coach, but there is an equal amount of negative aspects to the job too. If coaches do not handle these aspects properly, the stress buildup can be extreme and unhealthy. I hope this book opens up your eyes and creates a good picture about things the coach can do to make his or her season one of the best seasons ever. We all need growth and development, and I believe this book, ***Coach, There Is Hope***, will create a more successful year for all coaches at all levels. Please enjoy, reflect, and grow as you read this book.

-1 Hope-

Family First

Juggle Your Personal Life: Family or Those We Love Should Always Come Before Coaching

In 2000—in the middle of head coaching one of my high school teams—my mother passed away. I will never forget the day that the doctor told me not to leave because he was not expecting my mother to live long. In my mind, I never thought my mom would pass away at only 47. I knew that she was not doing well, but I just did not want to believe that it would be the last time I would see her alive. I was under an immense amount of stress and I had no siblings to lean on for support. As a result, I missed one month of work to finalize all of her affairs. While I was still in hot pursuit of my coaching dream, I had to let my assistant take over the team while I settled matters at home. In addition to the stress of my mother's passing, I was also very worried that my athletic director and high school principal would get tired of waiting for me to return. So not only was I out of a coaching job, but I was also in a poor position regarding my teaching positions in health, physical education, and drivers education. I will never forget leaving the hospital and telling my mom that I had to get back to work. She asked me to stay a little longer with her, but all I kept thinking about was all the work I had to do with the team I had left behind. I got on the highway to drive back to Virginia, only to arrive at 3:30 a.m. and get a call at 5:24 a.m. that my mom had passed away – I had to get right back into my car and drive eight hours back to

Pennsylvania. Unfortunately, I had to learn this the hard way, but family or those we love should always come before coaching. At that time in my life, I was in my late twenties and focusing on my coaching career. I often wish that I would have given my mom just a few more hours, as she had requested. I know that I could not change anything about her passing, but I wish that my mind would have been "family first" at that time.

I have had a lot of coaching friends share with me that they had to make a decision to drop out of coaching eventually because they were not getting enough family time. Most of these coaches have shared with me that they wish they would have been more balanced in how they managed their coaching jobs and family life. I wrote an article for the *Olympic Coach* that focuses on prioritizing family before coaching. I shared with the readers that you have to be intentional about prioritizing your family over your coaching profession. If not, situations can and will always steal your family time. There are a lot of things you can do to make sure you are prioritizing your spouse or children before your career. I know that your job pays the bills, depending on what level you coach. However, a job will come and go, but family will be there. As I shared my story about the loss of my mom, I hoped I illustrated the importance of investing time with whom we love. Therefore, I am begging coaches to prioritize their family before their coaching career. The coach can invite their families to participate in their practices, invite them to attend games regularly, or have them over the house for a meal or a cookout. I know that your job takes up an immense amount of your time, therefore, embrace your family to be a part of what you do. I know that this is not an easy task and you may have a spouse or significant other who does not support your career. It may have a lot to do with how you have gone about balancing them and your coaching profession. First, you need to ask for their permission to be a coach and then be truthful about the job requirements. Remember, you cannot expect your spouse or significant other to embrace your dreams if you have not made him or her a part of your initial dream. Therefore, ask your spouse for his or her input on certain coaching-related issues. Ask his or her support and let the significant other know that you don't want to do this by yourself, and you desire that they journey with you. Remember, that is what love does. It is not selfish; it is unselfish. Even for the single coaches, make sure that you find time to balance your life. I know that you are doing this all by yourself. It is hard to come home after a long game and not have anyone with whom to share your coaching successes or failures. It's tough having to take care of your home on your own, juggle your own bills, visit family and assist them when needed, all while trying to take care of yourself. If you are a single coach, just remember to live a balanced life and do not let people overwork you because you are single. I know how this feels, as well. There is a misconception that because you are single, you have time to do everyone else's work. WRONG! You may be married, single, have children, or have other relatives who are very valuable to you. Please make time for them—coaching will always be there for you or someone else when you return.

Hope Keys to Remember

- Prioritize your family first

- Ask for permission from your family to be as busy as you will be

- Invite your spouse or significant other on the journey

-2 Hope -

We All Have a Story

My Personal Story That Led to Stress and, Eventually, Burnout

In 1994, I started coaching an intramural basketball team. During that year, I transferred to another university to pursue my degree and basketball career. Because of a National Collegiate Athletic Association (NCAA) rule, I had to sit out a year before I could officially participate in my sport. In 1995, I had a college-ending injury, which led me into the field of coaching. As I sat on the bench watching my team practice and win championship games, I realized that I still wanted to be around basketball. I watched my coach, James Sweat (an NCAA Top 100 basketball coach), make plays, develop tape, recruit, travel, talk with parents, and develop his players into great decision makers. I loved the aspect of coaching and developed a greater desire to coach basketball. As a result, after I graduated in 1997, I took my first official paid coaching job with a middle school. As a young coach, I was unaware of the immense amount of pressure that was associated with being a coach. While I eventually went on to coach middle school, high school, and college, my middle school coaching experience was very unusual because my role as a coach was different. I was teaching full-time as a health, physical education, and family life teacher. At that time, my primary coaching goal was to help adolescent girls mature for high school.

My hope was that this could eventually lead them to an athletic scholarship. Even though I was juggling multiple roles and responsibilities, I was young and full of energy. I was at the start of my professional coaching career and I was beginning to see my dream as a coach come true. From the beginning, I was very passionate to see it to the finish line. I had some success that led to two out of three track championships and two out of three basketball playoffs. I loved what I was doing and did not experience the stress others may have experienced because coaching was my escape from the other stresses that came with being a new teacher.

In 2000, I was promoted to head coach of the junior varsity boys' basketball team and an assistant to the lead varsity team. The amazing part about this was being asked by the athletic director to coach this team. This was very exciting for me because I was a female coach who was coaching an all boys' junior varsity team. In all honesty, this was my favorite coaching job. I had no problems with male athletes, and they treated me with dignity and respect. As a matter of fact, coaching the junior varsity boys' team earned me the National Basketball Association/Women's National Basketball Association and the National Federation of State High Association's Coaching Sportsmanship Awards. Just this past summer, a few of my former athletes reached out and I had the honor to spend time with their families.

Unfortunately, the onset of stress slowly began while coaching high school basketball. I started to feel the pressure of winning from the administration and community. However, I was still passionate about my sport and the athletes, and I did not feel that it was time for me to move on to something different. In 2001, a wonderful opportunity came to me as a graduate assistant at a mid-major Division I institution. This is where the stress began to take a toll on me. I remember those long hours of juggling graduate school, teaching several undergraduate courses, 6 a.m. practices and workouts, summer camp planning, studying on the long bus trips, taking stressful exams, conducting class presentations, grading papers, and getting little sleep or not eating properly balanced meals. This went on for two years, and then I received an opportunity to take on a head coaching job as an interim coach at a small college. The stress increased when I became a head coach. I remember the pressure that I felt to perform, recruit the right athletes for my program, work with other coaches and administrators, juggle being a senior women's administrator, and deal with other job-related tasks.

Thankfully, another opportunity to coach and teach one course at another mid-major Division I institution presented itself. I took the job immediately! At first, this opportunity was great; however, stress began to kick in again as the job became more intense. I remember working on three to four scouting reports at one time, getting off the bus at 5:50 a.m., and getting back to the office at 8 a.m. to start my regular work hours. Again, I was getting little sleep and I was constantly either getting a cold or recovering from one. As a matter of fact, I had put on more than sixty pounds from the time I originally started coaching. In 2005, the sport that I once loved brought on such an overwhelming amount of stress that I became burned out, which led me to leave the field of coaching in 2007.

I'm sharing my story because I want to help coaches, especially younger coaches, become aware of the stress associated with the profession. Furthermore, I would like to see young and more seasoned coaches be more proactive in avoiding the dangerous traps of stress that can lead to burnout in coaching. As coaches at all levels, and especially college, we have to recruit, work long hours, fight to get proper sleep, exercise when we can, hire and supervise workers, be responsible for the athletes we are coaching, and juggle a personal life. As a result, I want to share the twelve components I wish I would have taken into consideration while coaching. Though I did incorporate several of these components at the time, I am now able to advise coaches about the aspects I wish I would have done differently during my coaching career. Several coaches have put these suggestions into practice and are getting better results. Remember, it is not only good to listen to what we need to change, but it is great to apply the things we can change even when the job begs for that which we cannot change as coaches.

Hope Keys to Remember

- Share your story with other new and more seasoned coaches

- Be aware of the dangerous traps into which stress can lead you

- Know what burnout looks like and avoid it

3 Hope

Recruiting

Recruiting: This Candidate is Not the Only Athlete in the World

It is a fact that if you are at the middle school, high school, and/or college level of coaching, you will have to do some form of recruiting. It is inevitable. Recruiting can be stressful because it usually involves several other programs to which other coaches desire to attract the same athletes. Recruiting has its high and lows. There are times when you will feel that you just won a particular athlete, only to find out that he or she decided to transfer to another school district, university, or professional team. When this happens, it is important for the coach to realize one key element: this candidate is not the only athlete in the world. I remember the times we would receive the call that the student-athlete had committed to another university. But as soon as I stopped focusing on the fact we had lost that recruit and began to put my focus on other recruits, we would end up signing another recruit who was equally talented. My point is that you have to learn to shake off the disappointment of the sought after recruit's de-cision. Furthermore, you have to make a decision to move on to the next athlete quickly. Try not to get frustrated and wallow too long.

Remember, student-athletes, professional athletes, etc., have the right to select where they want to spend the next few years of their lives. I know you put a lot of time, energy, effort, and even monetary expenditures into recruiting them with your school, university, or professional team, and this can be very disappointing. Where they spend their lives is a destiny decision and they need to select wisely. It is also important for the coach to select wisely, as well. If you are recruiting someone and you have to beg to come for a campus visit, beg him or her to answer the phone, beg him or her to respond to your emails, Facebook, etc., it is a strong indicator you will probably have to beg that person to come to your program. In most cases, these athletes are usually your problem athletes. These are the athletes who, once recruited, will continue requiring you to beg them to come to practice, beg them to get with the program, beg them to practice hard, beg them to conform to your rules and strategies as the coach. If they are totally ignoring you and keep doing the same thing over and over, this can be a strong indicator that you really do not need them in your program.

It is best to pull away when you start to see some of these same behavior patterns during the early recruiting stages. On the other hand, there are recruits who will sometimes shock you and reappear at the last hour. Therefore, my suggestion is to work hard, work smart, and use wise judgment in observing the personalities of your potential recruits. Moreover, the coach needs to observe what type of personality is needed for the overall success of the team. I always go back to

Coach Phil Jackson's strategies when playing his players. He had Michael Jordan, the scorer; Scottie Pippen, the passer; Dennis Rodman, the rebounder; and other role players who stayed in their lanes of expertise and basketball IQ. I know that Pippen could have easily been a scorer if he would have stepped out of his role. Such players showed the unselfishness of their hearts because they selected to do what is best for the entire team and organization. As a result, I feel it is truly essential to evaluate the missing personality pieces that are needed for the success of your team. This can minimize a lot of undue stress.

I feel that all teams need five types of players who can assist the coach in reducing or at least minimizing stress. The team needs a leader, a role model, an encourager, a *positive* counselor, and what I call the "all-outer". For instance, it is good to have a truly strong leader on your team, someone who is very vocal and will challenge athletes who are not producing to their potential. This can help reduce the coach's stress by allowing the leader to sometimes point out when other athletes are not giving their best. This generation of athletes does better when their peers challenge them because they are more likely to buy into their corrective feedback.

The role model sets the tone for the other team members to observe. It is good to pair up other athletes with the role model because they usually set the tone on how to conduct oneself and they can also provide positive feedback for the other athletes to adhere to if they are truly practicing what they are preaching. A role model talks the talk and walks the walk.

The next, and maybe the most important, person on the team is the encourager. I remember a young man who used to encourage from behind—which means, even though he was not the star player, or in most cases never got in the game, I would watch him encourage his teammates every time they were in and out of the game. Some players would even go straight to him, rather than the coach, when they would make mistakes. This athlete understood his role on the team and he did it well. Furthermore, I love how the coach allowed him to play his role. I said to myself, "This kid will make a great coach someday". Incidentally, he is now coaching at a mid-major Division 1 institution. This coach, who used to exercise his ability to encourage and motivate from behind at the end of the bench, had been preparing himself for his future coaching career.

The *positive* counselor is vitally important, as well, because he or she can provide and sometimes reaffirm things that the coach has already addressed. I emphasize the word "positive" because the coach can get athletes who are modeling the wrong negative counseling, which can add more stress for the coach. The negative counselor will only bring more division and discord to the team. Therefore, the coach must observe the positive counselor during recruiting. This person usually makes tough life decisions and is easy to talk with.

Finally, the all-outer is a must for every team. The all-outer is going to give everything you ask of him or her and usually without complaints. This is the athlete who goes after every loose ball, and goes above and beyond what is asked of him or her on the field or court. Sadly, in my observation, the all-outer is usually the athlete who, in most cases, is not your best player on the team. However, all-outers are most coaches' dream player and key role player.

Keep in mind, even though my five types of recruits can lead to de-stressors for your team, know that they are still human and will make a few mistakes. Give them room to grow and develop and find their way, especially if they are middle and high school athletes. Implementing my five types of recruits will not guaranteed you perfection, but I can tell you that you will reduce a lot of possible undue stress that you just do not have time for as the coach. Oh, and by the way, yes, they need to know how to play your sport. Recruiting is a job all by itself; therefore, you have to be very selective and wise in your choices.

Hope Keys to Remember

- This candidate is not the only athlete in the world

- Work hard, work smart, and use wise judgment in assessing the personalities of your potential recruits

- Identify the leader, role model, encourager, *positive* counselor, and the all-outer on your team

-4 Hope-

Long Work Hours

Long Work Hours: Prioritize and Work Toward Maintaining Balance

Dr. John Maxwell states in his leadership trainings, "Take care of yourself more than you take care of others." As a young coach, I did not hear this quote until 2003 and it was in a sport management graduate course. As a teacher and a coach, I was busy making everyone else better except myself. I spent long hours training and conditioning my athletes instead of working on myself, as well. In coaching, the coach has to be careful because he or she may be the first person in the gym and the last person to leave the gym. The list of job-related tasks can continue to grow. We all know coaching comes with long days. Some days the coach can leave the office early, and other days he or she will have to be there late into the night; in my case, I was even coaching mornings. This is where the coach has to prioritize and work toward maintaining balance. For instance, the coach knows that in the midst of the season, it can get pretty busy and monotonous. Therefore, when he or she has downtime, it is important to maximize those moments. This is the time to take a trip to a nice getaway, cut the cell phone off, and spend time alone or with people who will refresh and recharge you. It is important to have a calendar of planned rest times during one's season and even throughout the day.

As a college professor, I know the importance of taking little breaks. Sometimes, those breaks are just a small walk around campus or a visit to see a colleague who I have not seen in a while. I realize that much of life for most coaches is spent at work. Therefore, it is important to take necessary steps to create what I call "ME TIME." This "ME TIME" is your own little world of happiness. Coaches know they need to find time to balance life; however, at some point in our coaching careers, we might look back and realize we spent way too much time coaching. I do not want any regrets. I have seen a lot of coaches regret the amount of time they invested into coaching their sport and athletes. This time spent is a nice investment, and I will discuss more about the topic of caring; however, you can get so stressed out that it can lead to burnout. Coach, take time to invest and pour back into yourself.

Okay, we all know coaching is a demanding profession. We also know we really cannot do much about the hours; however, we can be intentional about prioritizing what really matters and investing our time wisely. For instance, if you have small tasks you can pass on to someone else, like your assistant coach, team manager, etc., then by all means, delegate responsibilities. When you do this, you create an open space of time (even if it's just five minutes) in which you can reflect, relax, restore, and recover some "ME TIME." Maybe you do not have an assistant coach, team manager, or any other supporting staff to whom you can allocate responsibility. Coach, if this is your situation, I suggest you consider finding some good volunteer coaches. Believe it or not, a lot of people just love the title of "Coach" and will do it for free—and, with proper training and support, can do it well. Most organizations will require you get clearances and a background check for a volunteer coach. However, this is time well spent because you'll get the help you need. We only have twenty-four hours in a day and we cannot change that; but we can change how we delegate and balance those hours. I also suggest you take time to get away and reflect on your season. Look at what and who is stealing your time, and make some adjustments. We all live and learn, and it is up to us to do something about the things we can change and not try to control the things we cannot change, such as having only twenty-four hours in a day.

Hope Keys to Remember

- Dr. John Maxwell says, "Take care of yourself more than you take care of others"

- Take a trip or getaway

- Turn off your cell phone and all electronic distractors

- Schedule planned rest time

- Create your "ME TIME"

- Delegate small tasks to your supporting staff

- Get more volunteers if needed

-5 Hope-

Poor Sleeping Habits

Poor Sleeping Habits: Look at Sleep as a Win and Not a Loss

Most coaches are used to long working hours, which can result in difficulty sleeping. After work, it is important to take your mind off work and begin to develop a "quiet time." The coach can use music, reading, or watching a fun movie to wind down from the stresses that can cause a lack of sleep. Some coaches have adopted the mindset that if they are resting or sleeping, they are not working. To be honest, in order for the coach to have a more productive day, he or she will need to focus on getting the required seven to eight hours that is necessary for our bodies to function properly. Therefore, it is imperative for the coach to look at sleep as a win and not a loss.

I have even heard coaches mention how they really require only four hours of sleep most nights. Well, according to most research, the average human needs between seven to eight hours. You may feel normal and rested, and a lot of that has to do with routine. This means your body will start embracing those long hours and start adapting to the schedule you have placed on it.

Due to this technological world in which we live, it is very hard to turn off one's mind. I have read several times that we have thousands of thoughts that shoot through our heads during the course of a day. I have also done a quick little observation for the last eight years in my class: I ask the students in the course of one minute to raise their hands every time a thought comes through their heads that is not related to what they should be focusing on in class. On average, hands start rising within five seconds of the beginning of the observation. This confirms we all experience mind overload. As a result, when the mind is on overload, it is hard to sleep. This, too, happens in coaching. It could be after a loss or a win that the coach will find himself or herself having a hard time getting to sleep. This scenario may be more common after a loss. Coaches can find themselves reviewing, time after time, what they wish they would have done to make things better or who they should have put into the game or the play that should have been called or, perhaps, the time-out that should have been taken. These are just a few of the thoughts that can cause the coach to lose sleep. One key element of a successful night of sleep is to cleanse your mind of toxic thoughts. These are usually negative thoughts about your season, a fear of failure, the pressure of winning, and the list goes on. This is why it is important to discuss happy moments and have happy thoughts before you go to bed.

As I mentioned at the beginning of this chapter about turning off your mind, the coach needs to do the best he or she can with being consistent in developing a sleeping pattern. I know during the season it can be hard to have a routine sleeping pattern. However, when the season is over, this is your time to embrace a routine sleeping pattern. I remember when we would get a few days off during the summer before the season. I would often take this time to go to the beach. One time I went with family, and I literally slept for three days. I did get up a few times to have bathroom breaks and eat very quickly, but overall I slept close to seventy-two hours. My family thought something was wrong with me and often came to the room to check on me. I was just tired and very sleep deprived.

If you have a hard time sleeping at night, try exercising and then taking a bath or shower. I promise this will help you fall asleep. I once did this several times, and I had the best sleep. A lack of sleep can cause a lot of stress on your body and mind. Furthermore, a lack of sleep can cause physical damage to the cells in your body. Also, when you are not rested, you are more likely to be irritable, forgetful, and unable to make effective, thoughtful decisions. Remember coaches, when you are more rested, you are likely to make better decisions that can lead to better outcomes and less stress.

Hope Keys to Remember

- Take your mind off of coaching and develop routine quiet time

- Discuss and think happy thoughts before you go to sleep

- Look at sleep as a win and not a loss

-6 Hope-

Lack of Physical Health Maintenance

Lack of Physical Health Maintenance: Good Health Produces a Better You

As mentioned previously, I gained more than sixty pounds before I decided to leave the coaching profession. Due to all the stressors that were associated with the job, I found myself handling everything else before I got a handle on my own health. I finally woke up one day and looked in the mirror, and took a closer look at how depressed and overweight I had become. I had slowly begun to lose the level of motivation I once had in my earlier years of coaching. I was constantly sick with either a cold of some sort of headache. During one of my regular doctor checkups, the doctor informed me my cholesterol was way too high. He also explained it was imperative I lose weight, exercise, and de-stress as much as possible. This was quite embarrassing because I was used to being the coach who was primarily responsible for the strengthening and conditioning of the team. I understood what I needed to do, but my focus was on my team and not my own personal health.

I see this happening time after time with coaches. I did a small study a few years ago and observed several coaches and their health. All of the coaches informed me their health had declined since they began coaching. Most people who do not coach have no true understanding how this can easily happen to the person primarily responsible for assisting others in their health. I can speak truly from the college coach perspective on how easy it is to put the pounds on and keep packing them on. It is simple. You work around the clock, which leads to the coach grabbing something quick, such as fast food, which leads to the coach not getting the proper sleep, which leads to no form of exercise or physical fitness. This can be true especially for former athletes who are now coaches. I remember having that wonderful athletic body as a young athlete. As a result, after I finished playing college sports, I did not exercise for almost five years, and I was still in top shape because I had trained my body for so long. It was amazing how I could just jump right back into running and sprinting without any pain or strain. If I try that now, I have to stretch for at least twenty to thirty minutes.

Coach, it is important you exercise at least three times a week. I call this self-investment, which means this is something you give back to yourself. It is important to value yourself and, when you invest back into yourself, you will feel much better investing in your athletes. Toward the end of my coaching career, I began to exercise and eat healthier. As a result, my cholesterol levels went back to normal and I dropped a few pounds, both of which made me more aware that good health produces a better you!

Hope Keys to Remember

- Don't let yourself go physically; get a grip before it becomes too late

- Invest in yourself by exercising and eating healthy

-7 Hope-

Hiring and Supervising

Hire and Supervise: Look for Trust and a Good Fit

I have heard many coaches share that hiring assistant coaches and support staff is one of their greatest challenges. The most recurring words I heard were "trust" and "good fit." Trust does not happen overnight, and it takes time for most of us to trust individuals. This could have to do with our past, our upbringing, and/or the betrayal of a close friend or loved one. Trust is a choice. Therefore, try not to shy away from or fear the hiring process. Sometimes, you have to be willing to take a risk on certain people until they show you something different.

I have found in coaching the importance of keeping yourself around like-minded people in the area of good ethics. This does not mean you have to think and coach the same; it simply means your psychological cores need to be similar. Weinberg and Gould (2007) define psychological core as your most intimate you, or the real you. A person's psychological core can come from one's family, religious beliefs, or teachings. When coaches look to hire, it is important they examine the interviewee's psychological core. Examining the psychological core will provide a good indication if you can look for trust, which can lead to a good fit. A good question to ask the interviewee is, "What is your coaching philosophy?" Have the interviewee explain and provide examples of how he or she has implemented his or her philosophy. Also, during the hiring process, develop an interviewing committee you know you can trust and with which you can share your deepest, most intimate fears or concerns. These people typically make up a good search committee because they know and have an understanding of your personality, which can lead to a good fit for your program. Sometimes it is good to not even be in on the interviewing process and make your internal selection before letting your search committee decide. It is very common for coaches to already know who they want to work for their program. They just need a little reaffirmation that they selected the right fit.

Also, it is good to remove yourself from making an emotional decision, especially if it is a close friend. I will be honest with you: it is very hard to hire friends. I have hired my friends on several occasions, and in some cases it turned out okay and in others it did not. It just depends on the maturity level of the friendship. I heard someone tell me that you do not know if you have a good friend or a true friend until you have a disagreement. No one wants to go out and start a fight with a close friend or close coaching friend, but the true test of a friendship, in some cases, has to do with how you disagree or fight. For example, one can fight properly and fight improperly. When you fight properly, you are able to resolve conflict in a healthy way that leads to a better re-lationship—as opposed to fighting improperly, which leads to more division. With this in mind, try to avoid hiring your friends as much as possible. If you hire the right friend, that is great; but if you hire a hard worker and someone who is knowledgeable and trustworthy, that is even better.

Hiring is one aspect; however, supervising is a whole other item to address. I know some good supervisors who are not good leaders and some good leaders who are not good at supervising people. This is why Chapter 12, which discusses accountability, is very important. You have to know your strengths and operate to the highest level at your strengths. It is good to get people around you who are better than you in certain areas where you may not be as strong. I used to think you needed to master everything as a leader until I realized that we are all good at a few things but not everything. Most of us never took a class on how to be a good supervisor, nor was it offered in most classes at the undergraduate or graduate level. Therefore, it is important to receive as much training as possible, or to take a class on effective supervising or leadership training. You want to be the supervisor for whom others enjoy working. This can only happen if you are intentional about developing yourself as an effective supervisor.

I can write another book on this topic because I am very passionate about leadership, management, and supervising. One concept I want to point out about supervising is to keep in mind that people do not belong to you. They belong to their spouses, children, siblings, families, etc. With this in mind, strive to be the type of leader who pushes others to go further than you have achieved. You, as the supervisor, do not have time to feel threatened or jealous when it comes to letting your assistant coaches or others who work under you take on a bigger and better opportunity for themselves. The goal should be to see them go far and learn a lot under your tutelage. I have worked for both types of supervisors, and I can tell you it is much better working under someone who will advocate for you and push you to greatness. Coaches, we all have an innate desire to excel in coaching and in life. Therefore, find people who are stronger, quicker, more knowledgeable, wiser, etc., in your circle or in your program. I am sure there will be someone on your team who you know could easily run your program without your direction or input. However, I am sure there is at least one talent or skill you can instill in this individual to make him or her much better.

I learned early in my coaching career that you are not ready to be in authority until you learn how to come under authority. If for some reason you are struggling in this area and not quite there yet with effective supervision, just go find help. Do not try to be something you are not *yet*. I emphasize "yet" because you can become a great supervisor once you intentionally work to grow in that area. Coach, just make sure you are equipping people from day one in your program to go higher and higher in their careers. Trust me, you will be surprised at how hard people will work for you when they know you want them to go far and achieve greatness. I can truly say this about my college coach, James Sweat. He has helped many of us go far in our careers and in life. He wanted to see us go further than he did, and he achieved much coaching success. Many of us are educators, doctors, and lawyers.

Remember, the primary goal of this book is to help coaches find hope in the potentially stressful world of coaching. Developing yourself and finding proper assistance in this area can make you become the supervisor you always desired to be. As a matter of fact, how good would it feel to sit back and watch all the people you helped develop over the years become great leaders? De-stress yourself at the beginning of the season and start investing in those in your program. Watch how much stress you will release when you put your mind to making another coach's, secretary's, or other support staff member's life much better.

Hope Keys to Remember

- Trust does not happen overnight, and it takes time for most of us to trust individuals

- Trust is a choice

- Sometimes, you have to be willing to take a risk on certain people until they show you something different

- Develop an interviewing committee you know you can trust and share your deepest, most intimates fears or concerns

- Try to avoid hiring your friends as much as possible

- Know your strengths and operate to the highest level at your strengths

- Get people around you who are better than you in certain areas

- We are all good at a few things but not everything

- Take a class on effective supervising or leadership training

- Be intentional about developing yourself as an effective supervisor

- Strive to be the type of leader who pushes others to go further than you have achieved

- Get people in your circle who are stronger, quicker, more knowledgeable, wiser, etc...

- You are not ready to be in authority until you learn how to come under authority

-8 Hope-

Caring: Constantly

Caring: Constantly

Another huge stressor associated with coaching is being responsible for those under your tutelage. When I think back on when I was a college head coach, I remember how stressed and worried I was as I ruminated in the middle of the night about one of my players or about one of their relatives. I would sometimes worry about how they were conducting themselves in public. I worked very hard at trying to make them responsible in their decision making with hopes they would make the correct, healthy choice. I then realized the more I showed my players I genuinely cared about them, the more they would think before they reacted. I know as a coach this may not always be true; however, it is important to show your players you care for them.

Furthermore, I truly believe caring can lead to a winning season. Yes, your team will need a few more very important aspects like talent, unity, and good coaching. However, try not to forget that caring is a key element, as well. So what does caring look like and how does it work? Caring can consist of many elements. For instance, I hear a lot of athletes tell me the coach doing the recruiting shared how much he or she cared for his or her athletes; but the coach demonstrated a lot of the opposite behavior once the athletes signed with the organization. Therefore, caring starts as a picture of consistency. Coach, it is imperative you be consistent in what you promise athletes. If you tell your athletes during the recruiting process that you will have the team over to your house for dinner at least a few times a month, then you need to have the team over a few times a month. I know the season gets busy and circumstances change. In this case, verbally communicate with the players that you would love to have them over, but due to time constraints, you are unable to do so. Moreover, express you will do everything in your power to have them over when thing slow down.

Another big complaint I hear athletes share a lot is the moodiness of their coach. This means they never know what to expect from the coach day to day. Several athletes have sat and talked with me, and have had breakdowns about the verbal abuse coming from some of their coaches. Coach, if this is you, please take time to listen to how you are making your athletes feel. You have to remember that a lot of these athletes may not be as mentally tough as you and I were when we were coming up. Furthermore, some of the athletes may have been told all their lives that they are nothing. Then they get to your program and you sell them a dream that you care, yet you say the same thing everyone else has told them over the years. You do not really know all about different athletes' upbringings. I am sure you have done a great background assessment on how they were raised, such as: Do they come from a two-parent home? Do they have a strong family support system? Are they ambitious enough to graduate with good grades and good majors that will lead to good jobs, etc.? However, you do not know what all athletes have had to overcome. I know you wish that they were tougher. I do as well. However, we live in a time when more athletes are coming from single-parent homes, have been around drugs, have seen domestic violence in their homes, and the list goes on. By all means, this will affect athletes' abilities to function and produce at the level of the coaches' expectations. As coaches, it is important to take all of those items into consideration. This is why we need more mentors and mentoring programs designed to encourage, challenge, and provide support for athletes who come from these different types of backgrounds. Athletes can succeed with the proper support mechanisms in place.

Coach, what I'm saying is that however you acted to get them into your program, just remember that is what they are expecting you to continue to demonstrate once they embrace your program. Mixed emotions occur when athletes are expecting one person and the same person shows up, but then acts differently from what was sold from the beginning to get them into your program. I know there is a difference between our coaching and daily practice demeanors; however, try not to let negative emotions destroy your team. I truly believe caring produces better teams, which can lead to less stress and more victories.

Hope Keys to Remember

- Coaches, be aware of how you are treating your athletes

- We need more mentors and mentoring programs designed to encourage, challenge, and provide support for athletes who come from these different types of backgrounds

- Athletes can succeed with the proper support mechanisms in place

- However you acted to get them into your program, just remember that is what the athletes are expecting you to continue to demonstrate once they embrace your program

-9 Hope-

Emotional Health

Emotional Health

Many highs and lows come with the profession of coaching. As a result, it is easy for the coach to get into distress, which is stress that is ongoing and can lead to possible health concerns. Emotional health is starting to be linked to many elements in the body. Such elements can include: high blood pressure, heart disease, and even some forms of cancer. It is amazing the amount of stress the average human is under; however, for the coach, it is the nature of the job. Coaches can find themselves extremely happy and rejoicing over a recent victory, only to receive a phone call later that one of their athletes got arrested or was seen drinking. Most people look at talking to a counselor as something negative. However, I beg to differ. We all need a neutral ground to revisit and examine our daily behavior. The coach could be lashing out at his or her players for more reasons than just the loss of a game. Just like athletes who bring their baggage to the court and field, coaches need to examine their hearts and intentions regularly to make sure they are experiencing healthy thinking.

Examining your behavior is very healthy and de-stressing. It is very toxic for coaches to think they are right in their own eyes. Let's be honest, as coaches, most of us think we know everything and we do not like anyone telling us otherwise. Coaches are used to directing others and pointing them in the right direction. As a result, it is hard to have someone redirect the coach. Therefore, coaches need to sit down with a counselor, pastor, mentor, close relative, or mentor coach at least once a year to reexamine how they are conducting their business or, even deeper, how they are handling themselves. Athletes often share with me most of their coaches were very emotionally unstable, and they never knew how their coaches were going to treat them from day to day. I do understand, coach, you are not going to be an easy-go-lucky type of person. Furthermore, your job does come with ups and downs that can create an atmosphere of being up and down. With this in mind, it is imperative you schedule regular times to meet with someone with whom you can be completely candid and express your innermost fears, concerns, and even regrets. This is not a sign of weakness; this is a sign of healthiness.

Getting frustrated and lashing out is under-standable from time to time in the coaching professional. However, it is not healthy for the coach to be lashing out every day. Every time the coach lashes out, he or she is creating more and more cortisol (the stress hormone) that is not good for his or her overall health. Coach, try to remember it is okay to get angry; however, it is not okay to continue to lash out on a regular basis. This creates a very unhealthy environment for your athletes to excel to the top of their game. Can you image a child who had to wake up every day wondering what his or her parents might do according to the parents' feelings? This would create a very insecure and fear-based child who would grow into a very controlling or even fear-based adult. The same is true in coaching. In order for your athletes to excel on and off the court and field, it is imperative you are creating an atmosphere free from unhealthiness and un-stableness. Remember, you are aiming for ways to de-stress, not stress.

Hope Keys to Remember

- Athletes share with me often that most of their coaches were very emotionally unstable and they never knew how the coaches were going to treat them from day to day

- Sit with someone once a year to examine your behavior

- Do not try to be right all the time in your own eyes

- It is not healthy for the coach to be lashing out every day

-10 Hope-

Avoiding the Arrogance Syndrome

Avoiding the Arrogance Syndrome

I realized it was okay to make a mistake during my first official game coaching college basketball. I knew I should have made a call but was a young coach and wanted to respect the assistant coach who had been there for years. I let him make the call, and I knew right then and there it was time for me to grow up. Deep in my gut, I knew I needed to take the lead and walk in the authority that was given to me as the interim head coach. I also realized I needed to apologize to my team for not making the necessary call when I had known better. To be honest, I had feared making the wrong call during the game as a very young coach. I had let a little fear and pride get in the way at this point in my coaching career.

I see this problem with many coaches. I know it is a hard pill to swallow when someone else has to tell you what to do. After all, you are the coach and you are used to telling others what to do. As I mentioned earlier in this book, it is important to learn how to come under authority before you can be in authority as a coach. Many coaches do not like anyone telling them what to do. I know this chapter is a hard one to read, but remember, I am trying to help you—and, for the most part, I don't even know you. Therefore, do not take it personally. I want you to embrace the art of humility. This means you are willing to be wrong from time to time; you are willing to jump in and do the dirty work that some of your assistants have to do; you are even willing to wash the clothes if need be. Never forget where you came from as a young coach. Be willing to be wrong. Remember, being right is way overrated. Also, when you start winning, please remember all those who went before you. Remember all the people and athletes who made this happen for you.

I see a lot of winning coaches get to a point where they look down at other coaches as if they have a disease. They will not talk with them, provide mentoring, or even offer feedback due to their arrogance. I encourage the winning coach to go even more out of his or her way to reach back and encourage other coaches to succeed. Congrats to you if you are used to winning! I am very proud of you because I know it does not come easy. However, take the high road and go out of your way even more when you are at the top. I often remember what Dr. John Maxwell said: "It can be lonely at the top so you may as well take someone with you up there."

Hope Keys to Remember

- Embrace the art of humility

- Remember where you came from

- "It can be lonely at the top so you may as well take someone with you up there"

-11 Hope-

Is More Really Better? (Practice)

Is More Really Better? (Practice)

One day before practice, I called my assistant coach in and asked him if he felt that we needed to switch up and do something else. I had begun to sense a little fatigue in my athletes, which can, in the long run, make them prone to injury. He was a little confused, but he agreed we needed to try something different. As a result, I took my team to a smaller gym and we did something totally different than basketball. We exercised to Billy Blanks's Tae Bo® routine. The athletes were soaked and dripping with sweat. They were all jumping up and down, exercising and having fun. I then realized it was important to switch up the mundane routine practice schedule from time to time. The next day's practice became one of the best practices we ever had. The players' energy was much better. Their focus was better, they worked as a team better, and they even imitated Billy Blanks the entire time on the court—all while accomplishing what we had asked them to perform at practice.

I understand your job can be on the line if you do not produce an immense amount of wins. This pressure can come from all levels of coaching: middle school, high school, college, and professional. It is important that coaches give their all to the profession; however, as I mentioned several times in this book, be balanced and realistic. I have heard many coaches say, "We cannot let other teams out-practice us." I do agree with this statement, but it is much better to not let a team outwork you while you are on the field or court. More practice, in some cases, could be the answer but in most cases it is not. It is more important to have productive and goal-oriented practices than to just do the same thing over and over again without any effective tools to measure your success. A lot of times we measure success only from winning the game. That is great, but you have to win one practice at a time. Coach, take some time to look at your practices and truly examine their effectiveness. Think about what you are trying to accomplish for that practice. Then set out to accomplish that goal, one step at a time. It may take you a week to reach one goal, but that is better than not reaching one goal the entire season.

Coach, I know it can be very stressful when you have to keep repeating yourself again and again and again. When you find yourself doing this time after time after time, it is then time for you to evaluate why the players keep repeating this same error. It is important to go back, review, and identify the problem. Once the problem has been identified, you can then begin to look at possible steps to the solution. Remember, if it is something the team has been doing for a long time, it may mean the players will need just as much time to correct the problem. I know you do not have a lot of time and an entire season to fix poor habits; however, you will need to evaluate and get to the root of the matter before you can identify the problem. This can take time, but with proper strategies you can and will come up with a solution. Again, this book is about identifying and locating things you can do to de-stress your coaching career.

Hope Keys to Remember

- Is more practice really the answer?

- Do something different

- Evaluate your practices

-12 Hope-

Accountability Coaching Partner

Accountability Coaching Partner

In life, it is always a good idea to have what I call an "accountability partner". I have accountability partners in all aspects of my life. Furthermore, I have two people in my life with whom I know I can share anything and I will not be judged or criticized. That does not mean the two people think I never make mistakes. It just means I know that I am loved no matter what mistakes I make. They have proven time and time again their love for me. These are two people who I have at the top of what I call my "Accountability Partners List." In coaching, it is important to always bounce ideas off someone who has more wisdom, more knowledge, and more insight than you. In most cases, these people usually have more experience than you do in a certain areas. This does not necessarily mean they are older but older coaches do, in most cases, have more insight.

Coach, it is possible to be practicing the wrong perspective for twenty years without anyone ever challenging you to think twice about some of your ideas and systems. I know most of society does not like change. I cannot say I always like change. However, change is necessary in order to advance. In coaching, all types of circumstances will arise: your athletes get pregnant or get someone pregnant, drink underage and get caught, make inappropriate videos—need I say more? Some of these cases you may not have experienced, but keep coaching a little longer and you will discover a lot you never thought you would have to address.

Unfortunately, we live in a very tough time in which athletes are under a lot of undue pressure from their peers and even sometimes their own family. As a result, you will need someone who is just a phone call away who can help you brainstorm effective decision making. I cannot begin to tell you how important this has been for me over the years. I still have a few of my coaching accountability partners who I can refer to others, as well. As a small side nugget, it is not only good to get a coaching accountability partner, but also other accountability partners in other areas of your life. Remember, you can use an accountability partner in the other eleven chapters of this book if need be. I know that can result in a whole lot of folks assisting and directing you. But you must put your pride down and be willing to admit when you made a mistake. We all do from time to time.

We live in a society that tends to only look at one mistake and highlight it. For some reason, you can do ninety-nine things great—but when you make one mistake, people tend to remember it over the ninety-nine great things you have done. I have found that when you make a mistake, be quick to admit it and ask for forgiveness. People will respect you much more than if you try to cover up the mistake. Also, it is good for your student-athletes to hear you say when you made an honest mistake. I am not saying they need to hear this every day; however, they need to see you are willing to own up to your inadequacy, just like they need to own up to theirs. This is why it is important to have an accountability partner who you can run ideas by before you make a final decision and later find out you did not think that decision through objectively and thoughtfully. It is much easier and less stressful to have your accountability coaching partner point out the mistake before you embarrass yourself with your team, parents, administrators, etc. This will remove a lot of stress from your life when your athletes can see that their coach is human just like the rest of the world.

Be willing to be wrong sometimes. Trust me, it is less stressful living a life of honesty than it is trying to maintain perfection. You will stress and wear yourself out trying to uphold the idea of being perfect. Therefore, release yourself and de-stress yourself.

Hope Keys to Remember

- It is always a good idea to have what I call an "accountability partner"

- It is possible to be practicing the wrong perspective for twenty years without anyone ever challenging you to think twice about some of your ideas and systems

- Let your pride down and be willing to admit when you made a mistake

- You can do ninety-nine things great; however, when you make one mistake people tend to remember it over the great things you have done

- Be willing to be wrong sometimes

Conclusion

My desire is that you continue to coach the sport you love. My book is designed to assist you in making a mind-altering change concerning coaching as it relates to stress. Remember, stress has a lot to do with how we view a particular situation and not the situation itself.

I wish I had known about the dangers of stress and burnout in my earlier years of coaching. If I had information like this before and during my coaching tenure, I would have been more proactive in the way I handled the stressors that eventually led to my burnout. However, I am grateful I have the opportunity to help those involved or who are interested in coaching learn from my experiences and lessons. As always, love the sport you coach! Please feel free to contact me if you would like further information at LaNiseRosemond@gmail.

Dr. LaNise Rosemond
P.O. Box 4192
Cookeville, TN 38502

Bibliography

[1] Smith, R.E. (1986). "Toward a Cognitive-Effective Model of Athletic Burnout," *Journal of Sport Psychology* 8: 36-10.

[2] Weinberg, R.S. & Gould, D. (2010). *Foundations of Sport and Exercise Psychology,* 5th Edition. Human Kinetics. Champaign, IL.

[3] Weinberg, R.S. & Gould, D. (2006). *Foundations of Sport and Exercise Psychology*, 4th Edition. Human Kinetics. Champaign, IL.

About the Author

LaNise Rosemond holds a doctorate degree in educational administration from Tennessee State University. She holds a master's degree in education with a concentration in sport management from Florida A & M University and a BS in physical education from Norfolk State University.

Rosemond is assistant professor in the Department of Exercise Science at Tennessee Tech University. Prior to joining Tech, Rosemond had been a head and assistant basketball coach at Division I and II institutions, athletic compliance coordinator, associate athletic director.

She is the president-elect for the Tennessee Association of Health, Physical Education, Recreation and Dance (TAHPERD), member of the North American Society of Sport Management (NASSM), National Coaching Association, and the National Speakers Association (NSA). She serves on the Sheriff's Citizens Strategic Advisory Council in Cookeville.

Furthermore, Rosemond runs a leadership program for undergraduate coaching and sport management students called the Sport Management Institute for Leadership Excellence (SMILE). Rosemond travels around the country giving motivational speeches to students, coaches, women, and people from all walks of life. She has given well over 100 speeches and has been a guest host on several radio stations.